CATASTROPHE THEORIES

OTHER BOOKS BY MARI-LOU ROWLEY

a Knife a Rope a Book
CatoptRomancer
Boreal Surreal
Interference with the Hydrangea
Viral Suite
CosmoSonnets
Suicide Psalms
Transforium
Unus Mundus

CATASTROPHE THEORIES

Mari-Lou Rowley

ANVIL PRESS // VANCOUVER

Copyright © 2022 by Mari-Lou Rowley

All rights reserved. No part of this book may be reproduced by any means without the prior written permission of the publisher, with the exception of brief passages in reviews. Any request for photocopying or other reprographic copying of any part of this book must be directed in writing to Access Copyright: The Canadian Copyright Licensing Agency, Sixty-Nine Yonge Street, Suite 1100, Toronto, Ontario, Canada, M5E 1E5.

Library and Archives Canada Cataloguing in Publication

Title: Catastrophe theories : poems / Mari-Lou Rowley.
Names: Rowley, Mari-Lou, 1953- author.
Identifiers: Canadiana 20220167826 | ISBN 9781772141917 (softcover)
Classification: LCC PS8585.O8957 C38 2022 | DDC C811/.54—dc23

Cover by rayola.com
Interior by HeimatHouse
Author photo by Dave Stobbe

Represented in Canada by Publishers Group Canada
Distributed by Raincoast Books

The publisher gratefully acknowledges the financial assistance of the Canada Council for the Arts, the Canada Book Fund, and the Province of British Columbia through the B.C. Arts Council and the Book Publishing Tax Credit.

Anvil Press Publishers Inc.
P.O. Box 3008, Station Terminal
Vancouver, B.C. V6B 3X5 Canada
www.anvilpress.com

PRINTED AND BOUND IN CANADA

The world of ideas is not revealed to us in one stroke; we must both permanently and unceasingly recreate it in our consciousness.
– René Thom

For Patti, Morgan, and Quinn

CONTENTS

PRECOGNITIONS

A Lesson in Dictatorship	13
Samantha, it's taken!	14
Out of Time	15
Duloxetine Dreams	16
Erasure	17
So Many Ways to Dance with Death	18
Preparing for Life on Mars	20
Slocan—The Mysteries	21
Finning awake	22
Don't leave your antecedents behind	23

CATASTROPHE THEORIES

Utility Program ▪ Alpha	27
L'amour Precession	28
Ode to Alan Turing	29
On Euclid's Book VII – Elementary Number Theory	32
On Diophantus' *Arithmetica*	34
A brief discussion on the evolution of tools and man	35
Fold Catastrophe	36
Cusp Catastrophe	37
Swallowtail Catastrophe	38
Butterfly Catastrophe	39

IF/GOD

What ever happened to Weltanschauung?	43
Daily Bread	44
Bye-bye Darling, Bye	45
Lone	46
Sight Unseen	47
Bald-faced Hornet	48
Bird Song Jet Stream	49
Space-Xd	50
Weight	51
Why Walk If You Can Fly	52
Bodily Selves	53

HYPATIA'S LAMENT / MARKOV ECHOLOGUES   55

Notes on the Text	87
Acknowledgements	89
References	90

About the Author

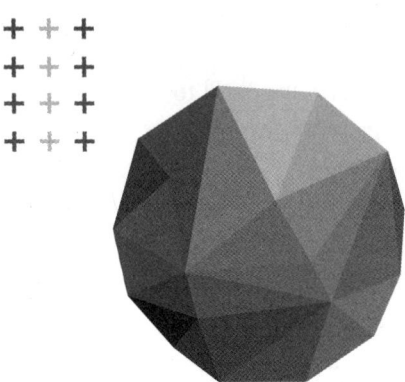

PRECOGNITIONS

A LESSON IN DICTATORSHIP

Inside the first-class lounge are two leopards, an old lion, and a man sleeping on the floor.

The leopards are affectionate but restless. The lion could care less.

As she enters, the leopards come up to greet her. One licks her hand, almost encompassing it.

They leave the man sleeping under a furry blanket on a pallet on the floor alone.

There are no flights to Zimbabwe that day. The leopards won't let her sleep or eat.

SAMANTHA, IT'S TAKEN!
DREAM PHRASE 1

It was there, under the bush, I heard it rustling but now it's gone. Perhaps a moment like ice before melting or a leaf before it drops. Or emerging from sleep and a dream of a pregnant ballerina levitating, the beautiful weight of two bodies hovering together in the air the moment before you awaken.

Or the muffled mewing of a small animal, a featureless furry creature abandoned or lost or running from the hunt. Or maybe it wasn't there at all, just a figment in time, or of time gone by so swiftly that we forget to look in the small places for questions or answers or whatever might be hiding there, lost and forsaken.

Do you hear that? A chirp or twitter, small phonemes of fear or frenzy. What you feel when the door slowly opens behind you and the hinge squeaks slightly and you know nothing is there but the voice in your head that breathes down your neck, a shrill little laugh behind your back when you turn to look but are mistaken.

OUT OF TIME

the way a fog-draped field veils the sun
luring wanderers into a mirage of whiteness

the way a dream reveals the enemy
in the guise of oneself

the way coffee smells the morning after
a late night and too much thought

the way the earth rotates under our feet
and we don't notice its slippage

the way the heart drums in the body
tirelessly, the way it feels when out of time

DULOXETINE DREAMS

A Roman dandy in purple boots guides us around the Basilica—
sculptures of Plutarch, Plotinus and the boys stare blindly as we pass.

High on the domed ceiling are painted frescoes under which screens
gleam down video installations sponsored by the financial district.

The stone scholars look miserable. *Wits but a wool gathering* they
murmur as tourists tweet selfies to increase their following.

In the Thermopolium customers in cashmere and kid leather wait
patiently as I try to decide between tuna or crab.

Women with lips Pompeian red suck cocktails through straws
in front of more frescoes of nymphs astride sea horses.

Somewhere a praeco booms out edicts atop marble steps, a prostitute
finds god, the devil finds a president.

Homeward on the wrong subway the echo of a grade-school bully
taunts and haunts.

ERASURE

expandable   expendable
hard disks   heart disks
discussion around the periphery
words tossed thoughtlessly
for the dog to catch
for groomers of the world
to brush to a seemingly wild and true
sleekness

a lone pickup along a grid road's westward meridian

meditate on white, facing west
to shrink the nodule on your lung

avoid cold drinks, news of wilderness
snatched for coal plants
all the torturers in our midst

wrap your body in wool and feathers
lie down in a sunbeam facing west
close your eyes to slits until all you see
is white
         erase yourself

SO MANY WAYS TO DANCE WITH DEATH
MUTATED DREAM PHRASE II

Tango with a gigolo
on the edge
of a lagoon
an accordion playing
in the bayou background
crocodile eyes
periscope
wait for the misstep.

Waltz on the ice
with a dancing bear
skate blades
cutting time to Strauss
which annoys the bear
as does music in general
if he charges don't think
you'll ever outskate him.

Fox trot with the Minister of Defence
he looks so silly
with those cumbersome guns
but you must not laugh
you must not.

Two-step with the President
be careful not to smudge
his shoes or hold his
clammy hands too closely
in case they misplace themselves.
Compliment him on his newest selfie
the advancing iceberg of yellow
hair but never ever on his double
chin/talk/deals.

Square dance with the head
of the oil company
and his PR staff
Do-si-do all around
the tailing ponds
in the moonlight
gleefully
light a match
throw it in.

PREPARING FOR LIFE ON MARS

In the dinghy the swells eclipse everything, including the final chapter. Despite this, she feels a tremendous sense of calm, inevitability shrouding her like a four-point Hudson's Bay blanket, red and heavy. The water is so oily you can walk or glide over it; even without a paddle she is able to reach the shore.

Meanwhile, spacecraft are landing on Mars in search of alternative environments. Here, also, shrouds are required. The Orion pressure vessel provides a sealed environment for astronaut life support in future human-rated crew modules.

For tour interviews, contact:

Bill, Mike, Mark, Scott, John, Steve, Mike, Rick, Mike, Jim.

For media and more information, contact:

Cheryl, Rachel, Tracy, Shannon.

SLOCAN—THE MYSTERIES
DREAM PHRASE III

It was somewhere near that mystical valley
a Valhalla of mountain lakes and high meadows
where small violet butterflies the colour of Liz Taylor's eyes
flit and dart the way her eyes must have when
she first met Mark, or Richard.

It was the day Elvis died and we were driving along
the highway that hugged the mountain and
I was glad to be on the inside. Love Me Tender
was playing on the radio and I remember
aunt Bernice taking me to the movie when I was three
and how I loved Elvis like a pretend father.

It was high on a plateau, outside Vernon,
where we pulled over near a stream to stretch our legs.
A sullen dread hung over the place despite the morning
brightness and it was then that I knew Slocan meant death.

He felt it too, my friend who feared nothing but this dread air
of danger that followed us past quaint-named places—
Rosebery, Retallack, Lemon Creek, Appledale, Winlaw,
Slocan Park—to this deserted highway rest stop.

Only years later to discover it was near here or someplace
like it—water running in a stream, the smell and prick
of pine needles or something larger, sharper
where Olson, Shearing, or Fowler killed their first victims.

FINNING AWAKE

Oh outbreath, blow hole Oh

whale fins gleam red under-sided
       finning awake

a wake, oh what a whale of a day/dream
they are finning and splashing

       wake up!

and the deer come out of the forest
out of the fire
onto the lawns and the fawns follow blindly
as all mammals will follow their mothers
for the milk
for the body
contact until the road widens into a freeway
and there are no
stop
signs

DON'T LEAVE YOUR ANTECEDENTS BEHIND
DREAM PHRASE IV

Churning in the loamy twilight,
they deserve respect, these ghosts.

Harbouring from the arduous climb—out and away
from who you were or what you want
to become.

Don't wear your ghosts on your sleeve—
moaning and pathetic—if you ever expect
to gain entry, reach the top, love deeply.

The difference between ghosts and antecedents
is timing. Split second decisions
made in the wrong or right moment.

You can either open the screen door, let the wasp out
buzzing into the day, in counterpoint to lawnmowers
and the guttural staccato of other light machinery

or fill the wasp trap with stale beer and watch
its frenzied attempts to escape drowning
while you sip chianti, turn the steak on the grill
as summer fades into fall.

Rejoice or regret. You decide.

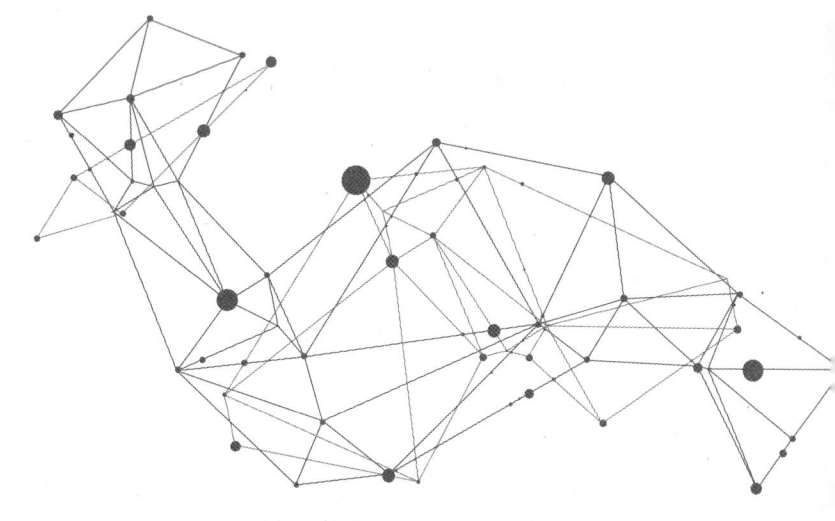

CATASTROPHE THEORIES

UTILITY PROGRAM ▪ ALPHA

This restlessness is a need to write down this restlessness ▪ Walruses stampede to the edge of receding ice floes ▪ Synapses tinged with embedded jingoisms, too much blubber ▪ What parts of the mechanism are you prepared to forfeit ▪

Amygdala dalliance in basal ganglia bandwidth, in the bling of an eyelash, detached from seeing ▪ Multiheaded daemons monitoring changes in host states ▪ Blink once to acknowledge federate clusters ▪

Back on the ice floe walruses fin the water, monitor changes in hostile states when the dictator bares his chest ▪ In the grand schema Web profiles are small utility programs ▪ To escape the cluster nodes, go out. Look up ▪

L'AMOUR PRECESSION

A comparatively slow gyration
        formerly
        in Platonic years

the intimate relationship
between space and time

        [Nutation]

            The sway and nod
            in the axis of rotation
            the invisible pull
            of pelvis
            to heart

    Now
heightened energy states:

            excitation and flux
            the interaction between text and touch
            digital kick or caress

Small magnetic moments
stored in the cloud
                a sigh, a sob

echo delay

        [The outer product of the wave function
        with itself]

ODE TO ALAN TURING

"Whether to move to the left, move to the right, or stay in place."

Unfamiliar odours of coriander, turmeric, cinnamon
what they brought back from that dark place
what they left you to face, alone
        with only numbers
what counted, only numbers could decide
        proof or falsity
statements of love or hate.

*"In order for an animated machine to compute the world
you need real numbers in binary form."*

What tables of behaviour, symbols, squares
behind eyes closed tight behind tight fists.
No general process for determining whether a given father
is satisfactory or not.

Someone has to make a decision procedure
        oh oh oh one one one oh one oh one
        dot oh one dot oh oh one one

Oh Cambridge prestige and diction—
Oh Princeton money—Oh mock Goths—
Oh slippery climb up the tower—
Oh Dot Dot Oh!

One war, one woman, one Enigma
the probability of failing her, of falling
through the cracks, of cracking the code.

Oh computable numbers, your subjects and predicates
their sequence of symbols, machine sung—

DADDCRDAA; DAADDRDAAA; DAAADDCCRDAAAA;
DAAAADDRDA;

Hide the Queen's medal in a box. Move to the next square.

"The behaviour of the computer at any moment is detemined by the symbols which **he** *is observing, and* **his** *'state of mind' at that moment."*

Certain codes and mannerisms
immediately recognizable
the flick of wrist
inflection of voice
turn of head
colour of scarf
cut of suit.

"The state of mind of the computer corresponds to an m-configuration."

M for machine, for mother, for man—
the room scanned
glance exchanged
meeting arranged

compatible numbers converge computably
mutable, mutual programming
a condition of functions and definitions.

*"Turing believes that machines think.
Turing lies with men.
Therefore machines do not think."*

Suppose a cog in the wheel, a
tape in the machine, a bug
on the wall.
Suppose his strong hands, dark hair
thick vowels, hard thighs.
Suppose mutual compatible increasing continuous
satisfying sighs.

Suppose someone is listening.

ON EUCLID'S BOOK VII – ELEMENTARY NUMBER THEORY

PROPOSITION 8

If a [daughter]$^\alpha$ be the same parts of a [mother] that a daughter subtracted is of a mother subtracted, the remainder will also be the same parts of the remainder that the whole is of the whole.

only if the same parts
numbed and subtracted
a daughter fending
a mother abstracted

      a remainder

only a fraction, a decimal
half mooned, half sister
half life
somewhere
someone
else

      a reminder

does she look like him/me?
what secret folds of history
pieces of pocket fluff
remainders of the whole
that is a hole

a number subtracted
from a number subtracted
one minus one equals
nothing left
to give her/us, just
reminders of nothing
holes in the whole

α Where the words [daughter] and [mother] replace Euclid's word [number]. The ancient Greeks had no numerical notation, so they wrote out formulae in text.

ON DIOPHANTUS' ARITHMETICA
after Paul Dutton

A "wanting" and a "wanting" yields a forthcoming.
A "forthcoming" and a "wanting" yields a wanting.[β]

and did I tell you over the brim of it all
and the words welling and sucked back
under the undertow of wanting to yield
all needing under your kneading hands

and the words welling and sucked back
and forth and finally returning to source
stream-head bubbling a fissure forceful
wanting your hands there forthcoming

under the undertow of wanting to yield
and fall forward running toward your
words outstretched and spilt forth over
the edge of this forthcoming yielding

under your kneading hands all thoughts
full of words unsaid re-verbed undone
this pounding ribbed throbbing wanting
and did I tell you over the brim of it all

[β] Where positive terms represent a "forthcoming" and negative terms a "wanting."

A BRIEF DISCUSSION ON THE EVOLUTION OF TOOLS AND MAN

A stick ceases to be just a stick when directions are drawn.

Once she scrawls his name on the wall, the tool is complicit.

Put a hammer in a hand and it can make or break things.

The #hashtag is mightier than the sword//joystick//pen.

Algorithms for data smoothing, the better to see (into) you my dear—
- aneurisms
- crumbling bones
- malignancies
- shrinking brains

The ghost in the machine—
- the programmers' dark desires
- the greedy need to see oneself on the wall of the other

Machines have intentions of their own anyway.

NaoV6 wants an orgasm and a Swiss bank account.

FOLD CATASTROPHE

after René Thom

Dilemma: *When vexed to extremes, stable and unstable pairs annihilate at the fold bifurcation.*

Elucidation: Bad branching behaviour in extrema. Mood swings from tree to tree. Back and forth these unstable pairings are volatile and weather dependent. Particularly when mating is technologically generated. Do you want to meet for coffee? A drink, perhaps, before bifurcation in the living room. Resolutions no longer palatable. Let's dance until foam rises from our mouths. Until our particles decay. Until we disappear. Until the story ends.

Formula: $V = x3 + ax$

Notation: Where V is the magnitude of vexation, x the vexee and a the vexor, who ultimately gets axed.

CUSP CATASTROPHE

Dilemma: *Under moderate stress a dog will exhibit a smooth transition of response from cowed to angry, depending on how it is provoked. A yell, a kick.*

Elucidation: To drown out the barking dog you turn on the news. Politicians baring their teeth. If overly provoked, once in angry mode they remain angry, especially when the war ends. Fabricated fluctuations in supply and demand result in market frenzy. To drown out the shouting, you walk the dog. While appearing to smooth surface behaviour, increasingly unstable warriors eventually meet and annihilate. This push of the button, flick of the switch is known as the tipping point. At which point all dogs turn and bite the hand that feeds them.

Formula: $\quad V = x_4 + ax_2 + bx$

Notation: Where V is electoral victory, x propaganda, a the politician, and b the loudness of the dog's bark.

SWALLOWTAIL CATASTROPHE

Dilemma: *In the schoolyard perimeter the paper plane is made up of three surfaces of folds, which meet in two lines, which in turn meet at a single swallowtail bifurcation point. Then it crashes.*

Elucidation: It's one thing to see a stuffed polar bear, moth-eaten and dusty, its neck wrapped in beads and a silly hat on its head, another to meet a real bear in the woods while oblivious to territorial claw marks but open to surreal wilderness experiences. Yet another to have your photo taken on Dali's lip couch in the courtyard of his villa under the scorching Costa Brava sun with the Michelin man standing guard. And later, alone in the swimming pool at the modest hotel observing wave patterns, angles of index and refraction, minimum-maximum pairs, and wondering about lost chances when a swallow dives just above your head fanning its tail as if to say, Follow me! What have you got to lose if you go with the dark Basque stranger to his parakeet sanctuary in the dusty hills? Your heart, your life, your plane ticket home?

Formula: $V = x5 + ax3 + bx2 + cx$

Notation: Where V is the tip of the Swallow's tail, x the object of attraction, a the direct route home, b the branching behaviour, and c the traveller.

BUTTERFLY CATASTROPHE

Dilemma: *At the butterfly point, two trains collide—spilling people, oil and grain. The reporters flock and then disappear, leaving a charred town, old news.*

Elucidation: So much depends upon the weather, a red wheelbarrow, and initial parameter values. How chaos is managed when a freeway collapses or a train derails depends upon where and what. City, country. Oil, grain. Wrinkles in the meteorologist's jacket belie conspiracy—small thermal fluctuations, the hush of a butterfly's wing. Exponential catastrophe from local minima. At which point, internet oligarchs buy fighter jets. Ask around at cocktail parties, "Say do you know any pilots who can teach us to fly these things?" At the butterfly point, tweets eclipse birdsong, greed trumps food and pandemonium exalts terrorism. Outrage swells fear as swallowtails soar and disappear.

Formula: $V = x^6 + ax^4 + bx^3 + cx^2 + dx$

Notation: Where V is the magnitude of chaos, a the media, b the oligarchs, c the fighter pilot, d the train engineer, and x the weather.

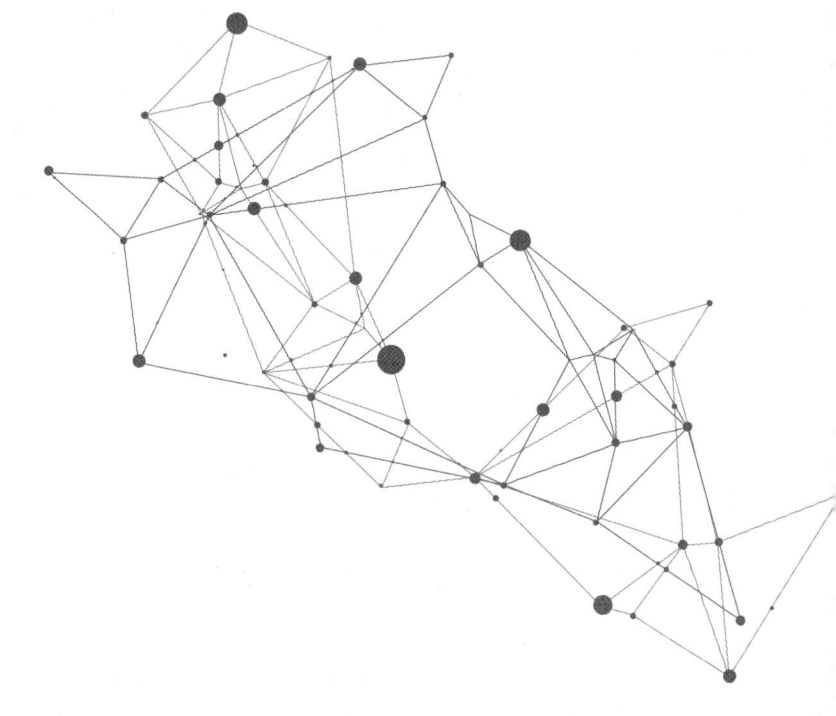

IF/GOD

WHATEVER HAPPENED TO WELTANSCHAUUNG?

You know, that old guy with the white beard
white socks and sandals even in winter who
went on about the big picture, the world
as a whole.

Meanwhile tiny estuaries in the left frontal lobe
leak words forgotten before we can remember
signals awry with jumps in syntax
digitally generated

and lousy wowsers on pedestals with wireless
mics, laser pointers aimed at abundance
proclaiming the right to drive
Hummers.

Meanwhile drilling, fracking, boring
cracks in the metal, manifold, mantle,

holes in the soul
seepage from the whole.

DAILY BREAD

The acropolis emerges in the hazy distance.

On closer inspection the dwellings are warren-like
homogeneity swept clean of history
except for noisy plumbing.

The people inside are starving
for something.

She sways her hips as she climbs the hill
stirring dough in a metal bowl.

Saviours come in all shapes and sizes.
If no fish, there is always bread.

Little boys scamper away laughing
arms laden with loaves.

On the freeway people in cars whiz by blissfully.

From the back of the bus the acropolis recedes
in one-point perspective.

BYE-BYE DARLING, BYE

In the hospital washroom behind the reception desk a woman is talking on her cell phone to her daughter. She has a northern English accent, Yorkshire perhaps.

The breast specialist found nothing suspicious but yes, dense, very dense the MRI confirmed. They ran out of gowns. The robe was green, the colour of trolls, and came down to my ankles. The staging diagram on the wall showed different lumps and masses—in situ, invasive. Stage I, hope. Stage IV, goodbye. How the breast is the organ of nurture and desire.

"Bye-bye darling, bye," the woman on the phone says. Remembering my mother, a rush of longing in my breasts that are fine now but oh how I miss her. Oh, how I want someone to call me darling again.

LONE

even with the sun setting over the lake on this chilly August evening, the scrubby poplars silhouetted against golden ochre and grey clouds interrupted by strands of fading blue

even with the hum of the refrigerator and the buzz of the one fly that won't leave and the grey gull passing

even with the fading laughter of children nearby and the sun lowering still and the stillness settling over the lake as the compressor silences and the leaves rustle

even with the incessant tinnitus hum in my right ear and the gull again

even with this lone body pulsing in the darkening twilight

SIGHT UNSEEN

Let's just pause for a moment. When we speak
like this the wind stops howling and grit no longer
stings our eyes. Although there is that shadow of
detachment, that detached curtain of viscous, that
wary window of lost opportunity, that bellow
of resentment, that glow in the dark, that warp
in the glass, that hollow ball of heavenly light,
that shift in perspective while walking through the forest.

What is discarded becomes treasure or trope. Like
the problem with blindfolds is they smudge mascara.

BALD-FACED HORNET

the hornet is on the arugula leaf
the same leaf as yesterday

perched and vibrant skull-faced broach
Dolichovespula maculata

not quite sure what to do—
needs a castle in Transylvania

or somewhere with urban angst, not this garden
this prairie city, beets and peas and cucumbers

troughs and crests of summer slipping away
the slow dizzy dying out, sting is gone

BIRD SONG JET STREAM

Glimpses of morning. Glimpseglimpseglimpse, nuthatch noise. Perfect bird language—such awkward English. Crows call overhead. Awkawkawkawawwwwk.

Birds bicker at the feeder. Fighter jets etch the sky with lace. No—beware of used-up metaphor, overextended lace. More like

Egyptian blue embossed with white, except more copper oxide in the blue more smoke in the white.

Forest fires rage, evacuees run, smoke smudges out the sun.

I was going to write about the mystique of flight. Take-offs and landings. Soaring above the clouds. The push of wind under wings. Thrust and drag.

Old photo and bones. Amelia Earhart's laughter, distress calls caught in the tail wind.

Back at the feeder, chickadees and nuthatches land and lift-off. Birdseed a bumper crop. The cat waits by the fountain for the birds to drink.

SPACE-XD

Thinking about birds
                                  and wires
       flight trajectories
missiles
               satellites

geostationary versus low shallow 5G orbits

thousands of gestapo spacecraft marching across the night sky
       Mars and Pluto conjunct in Leo in the tenth house
             communication versus Convenient Surveillance

puffy clouds of lost language
thoracic videogame bone pain

thumbs numb
               tongues dumb.

Who will Pay for all this Access?

Who will miss Betelgeuse—Orion's flaming shoulder
               going supernova

the cool swirl of aurora
       Venus's adoring gaze?

WEIGHT

of thought, of the body
bending, of berries
bending the boughs
of ash, red berries
somewhere between scarlet

        the colour worn by cardinals
        to depict blood
        and sacrifice

and carmine
saturated beyond standard gamuts
the extreme spectral red
of crushed scaled insects

        cochineal extract used in
        candy, lipstick, red fruit juice
        often anaphylactic

WHY WALK IF YOU CAN FLY

With a leap so light just lift yourself
   up
like a leaf, like a dancer.

Gentle thermal inhale and exhale
of the body's rise and lowering
into a cradle in the rock, wind break
resting place, belvedere
   sentinel control.

Oh the view from up here!
The scampering baroque adagio and arpeggio
of voices, towers, cities
   rising, falling.

Look! Over there—
small humans hide in a bush
over there—
a river quivers with the wrong kind of fish.

Turn your head to the right. Particulate haze
of a lazy afternoon, burgers and beer
   wild fires.

BODILY SELVES

Morning, late coffee and Kate Bush
the harpsichord perfect for sweet Bertie.

Out in my robe, cowboy boots
in the frost-wet, near-dead garden
solemn grey light
incanting the day
a hunkering down
fur thickening.

Pupils dilate as the day shortens—
as all we animals prepare
for winter.

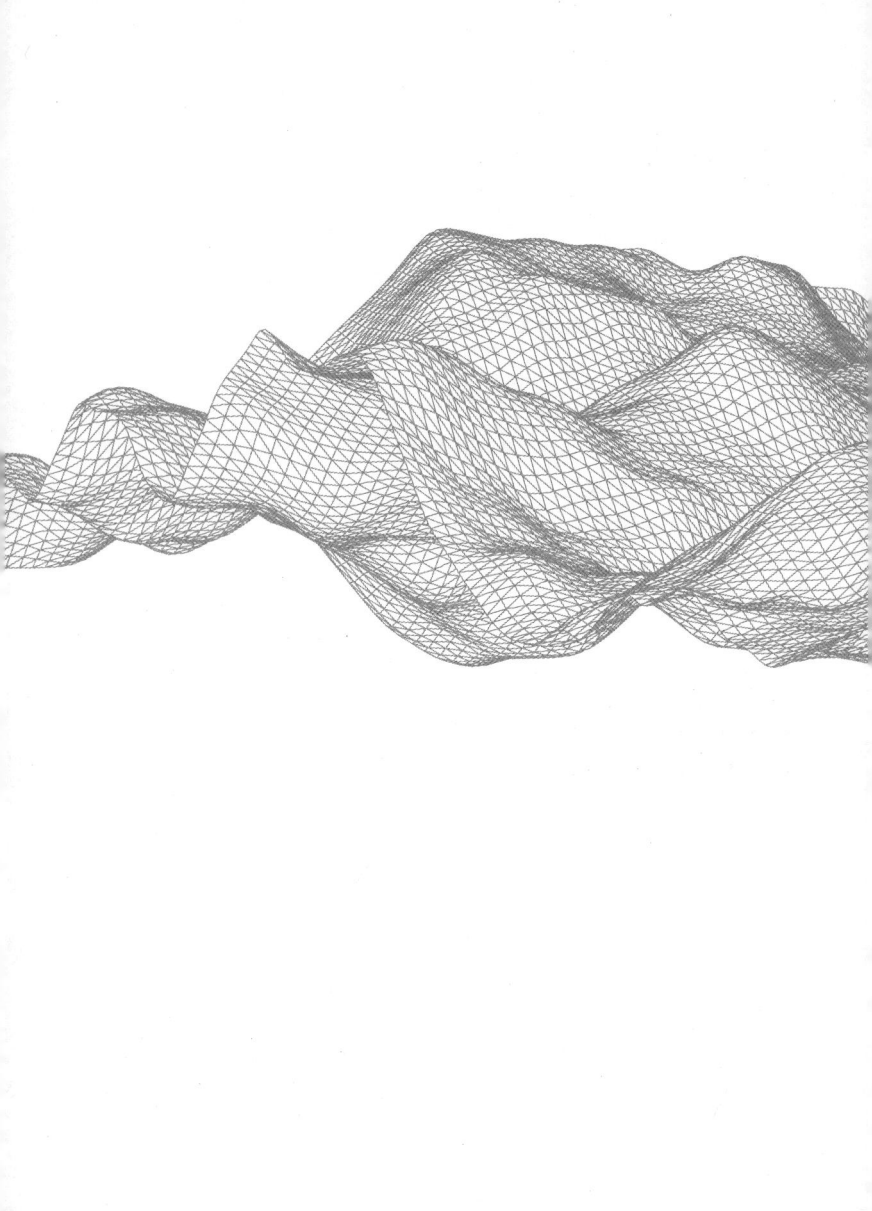

HYPATIA'S LAMENT/
MARKOV ECHOLOGUES

Life is emergence, the mind opening,
yearning to discover patterns in truth.
An unbridled thing, in need of harness,
cool philosophy and warmth of numbers.
Take my hand, for instance, or shell out-held,
how many drops of rain can they contain?
Then again, how many drops in a cup
before it overflows or is quickly drained.
The consequence of knowledge is danger;
the consequence of truth is not beauty.
To bleed a body dry, how many cuts
before thought takes flight in semblance of wings,
black against white, smoke against clouds, together
unfurling a holy chorus of rage.

A shell in hand
       is a shell in flight
is a shell fight
       of cool cuts
many flows
many hands

   Life in
     danger patterns
      shell flight as
    shell fight
      is a
thought as in
truth before opening before

consequence not knowledge

beauty needs
   consequence
      a can of
white emergence

clouds rain
the thoughts in

      smoke   in a shell fight
is the thought drain

the stance of wings
     is the thought
is
    flight

Unfurling a holy chorus of rage
in the rips and folds of my garments, skin
pale as a rare scroll it unrolls and burns.
Theon, my father, we yearn for the one
marvellous lemma, indivisible
as melting ice, life's subtractions and sums.
For the reason we hold knowledge sacred,
allow thought to soar above spires, unholy
ghosts and pyres cindering bone to dust.
To know the ebb and flow of tides and moons,
the curve of the sun in the palm of earth,
turn and spin of the celestial dance,
conjoining and conflict of the gods, all
immaculate knots and bone spurs of thought.

Pyres soar and soar and soar
      tides turn

  Too marvellous
the all reasoned thought
     rare and unholy

  sums soar   scrolls burn

      subtraction spires
a soaring of we
  melting lemma
     unknown
unrolls
     cindering reason   all
  thought rare as
    life

For knots melting knowledge
    we
      melting

Spires soar to the chorus
     skin
       in the dance

     ice garments dust bone
indivisible conflict of we
     melting

  lemma unrolled cindering
knowledge indivisible
  melting of life's
    For

Immaculate knots and bone spurs of thought,
ideas cohere and stir me awake.
The abstract delicacy of numbers,
their chaste and constant treble and timbre
linger like sparrow song on the day's dust.
Before being and empty space succumbed
to the *wet nurse of becoming*, water
was winnowed from air, from earth, from fire.
Before the four elements found their place
in the cosmos, ordered as they were by
ratios and sums, means and curves, beguiling
as a circle rolled and severed, radial
irrational in the phosphor of *pi*,
vital as fire is to the body's blood.

Empty
>   from constant becoming
water and blood
>   phosphor treble

   Is abstract as
awake numbers awake
   numbed bone to the
  phosphor of
becoming

cohere the severed body's vital
>   cosmos   on spurs

 Immaculate
>   rational nurse
>   delicacy in winnowed
>   song sparrow

The severed
 blood as becoming and
>   thought fire beguiling

earth-fire
>   rolled in sums
  pi
>   and ling

   Before
being and delicacy
   in winnowed
  song sparrows
cohere

Vital as fire is to the body's blood
drop upon drop, dust motes of numbers,
monadic exhale organizing space
and time, the horizon line between earth
and sky, a parabola of thrown stone.
How the angle of the sun can reveal
the size of Earth, the smooth trajectory
of planets wandering through the night sky.
A curve of metal focusing sun's rays
into a spearhead of light, blinding the
enemy, curling tongues of fire against
the gate, ballista of stone battering
moats and towers. Our dire transformation
of wisdom to weapons, fire to desire.

A parable
of horizon butting earth
against sky

towers phallic radiance curve

How the blood of the blood of our wisdom
arms against the sun's angle
    reveals
the line of light
  that dazzles itself
rotates the smooth orbit of planets
        wandering

How only exhalation of
    desire transforms fire
       tongues of
horizon between
  earth   and   towers
      phallic radiance curve

  How the blood of the stone that flew
that radiance curve

      How the stoned
    stood against the stones that flew

       How the
sun's phallic radiance organizes space
     and time   the night sky
  a parable of our wisdom

  Arms fire against the line
     of horizon between earth and
phallic towers

Wisdom's weapons become fire's desire.
Lance shafts waft in the change of gods, waiting
to be swayed this way or that, hallowed art
of rhetoric just another old trick.
Pluto conjùnct Leo in the tenth house,
omen for someone called Hitler one day.
Future too dark for any foretelling.
Astrologers' maps of transits and trines
usurped by sacraments, wine into blood,
bread into flesh, resurrection of souls,
and virgin birth. Women's slow sway disdained
by priests who hold our bodies at bay. Hail
hypostasia, swallow the holy host.
Three become one equilateral trick.

Of gods   waiting
      to be swallowed

Of rhetoric
     just another old holding
bodies at bay
              Hail
  hypostasia
that hallowed sway
that hollowed art
     rhetoric swayed
this waft in the hold trick

    Wisdom's resurrection
  usurped by sacraments
this waft in the hold of our bodies

  Hail hypostasia
    swayed in the hold
       in the tenth house
Pluto conjunct Leo
   in the change of souls
       trines
usurped by sacraments
wine into sway   hallow
   the holy host

Pluto conjunct Leo in the holy host

      Future too dark for any
sacraments

Three become one equilateral trick—
maidenhead, godhead, ghosthead. Senses
distilled through the shadow of encounters,
abstraction's alembic sieves impressions
into idea, the beauty of squares,
Pythagoras' hypotenuse of truth.
Consider, Synesius, the simple
symmetry of his seeing. Comprehend
if you can, divine triangulation
without proof. An alerion without
talons or beak, just wings to fly blindly
into the rank infinity of hell.
Reason trammelled by frenzy-seared souls
while a hypocrite sun glints off chalices.

Triangulation
   without
      talons or beauty
  of encounters
abstraction's alerion
   without proof

     grasp
if you can
  divine alerion
     without proof

An alembic sieves impressions
  into the
     simple symmetry
    of hell

Reason trammelled
  frenzy-seared
into the rank infinity
     of abstraction

An alembic
  sieves
impressions into idea
    the rank infinity of
his seeing

  Comprehend
    I

Hypocrite sun glinting off chalices,
how heavy to draw that cup to these lips,
denounce Apollo, Helios, with each
swallow. Does a name diminish their warmth
on the earth, the drawing of seed from soil,
or song from the throats of women and birds?
Instead of prayer, holy inquisitions
cleanse the air, purge minds of contrary thought.
What mysteries are greater than the mind?
Quadratics of parabola, the glimpse
of infinity in a spiral conch,
the harmony of perfect limbs, the hands
ability to sculpt them out of stone—
gifts of reflection that render beauty.

Chalices
how heavy
  to sculpt the mind

Quadratics of stone
      gifts of stone
    gifts of
       women and birds
    instead of
        stone

gifts of seed from soil
  or song
from
     soil
  or song from
their
warmth
  on the earth
     these lips

Does a name diminish in the air
        quadratics of prayer
              holy in a spiral of contrary thought

What cup to sculpt
the earth to these lips
denounce Apollo, Helios, with
     each
   swallow

Gifts of reflection that render beauty
as sand and water give way to wind,
the sway of waves, cycle of moon and stars.
Azimuth aligned with almucantar,
an astrolabe's tender mechanisms
track wandering planets, reveal the time
of day or night, the height of mountains from
earth to peak, etched against turbulent sky.
Smoke clouds our vicarious squints. How we
cradle grief as the library burns, ash
in the eye a strabismus of the soul.
Myopia and thunderclouds, knowledge
lost. Yet, Diophantus, your integers
console me, tantalize like wine, like tongues.

From
    earth
        from wind
squints the time
   of day
       or
  night   the soul
in the wind
      the sway
to peak   etched against
      earth

    Myopia and thunder mechanisms
track wander clouds

      tantalize like wind
   the soul

How we
     cradle grief
day or night   as the
library burns

  ash
in the ash
of day of moon of thunder

How we
    cradle grief as sand thunderclouds
our
   vicarious
      squints

Integers tantalize like wine, like tongues
relishing the taste of exotic fruit.
Ah, Synesius, to be pricked awake
by an angle's sharp point, compass's curve.
That things known can equal things unknown
and some equations can never be solved,
like Eros or Pythagoras' theorem
when the surd's power is greater than two.
Mathematics a dark foreshadowing
of power in matter and energy.
Enthralled by its simple perplexity,
Fermat scribbled in the margins of his
genius. Others scratch and claw at proof,
while I hold your head in my lap and sing.

I hold your
   head
         in the margins
of exotic fruit

   the surd's
power in my lap
         and some equal thing

That things
     known can equal
things
  known can
equal things unknown
       can equal

         the margins of his genius

Others scribbled

Fermat scribbled

Fermat scratched
       and sang

Mathematics a dark foreshadowing
         of

While I hold your head in my lap and sing—
meniscus of longing, the crescent moon's
articulated disk, this wrist, this knee
limpen with the tidal pull. Tantalus!
Such web, tow of desire. Something given,
something taken. The dull null aggregate
of one lone god inflames the creeping hordes.
Scarlet with sanctity they come for me.
Let me walk out to the receding lake
chains binding my hands, stones tied to ankles
plum in my open mouth. A million cuts
too many to count, to die by. Logos
is lost on lost souls. Words made flesh, to husk.
The trance in transcendence is all they know.

Ankles plumbed
       to stones
walk out
      walk out   entranced

In hands
  stones come for me

Let me
walk out
  plumed in trance

      stones in my lap and singing

    meniscus of longing
   the creeping
  given
something creeping

Hordes scarlet
    withering   they come

    Let me walk out
walk out
   they come for me

let me walk out to the
      crescent moon's
articulated disk

one lone longing
     transcendence
  tranced

Entranced by transcendence is how they know
an all-knowing god devised by priestcraft
for the purpose of power. A welter
of sarabites do their bidding. Finite
truth yields top-heavy ratios, un-towers
Babel stone by stone, roof tile by roof tile.
And bastard reasoning begets *pistis*—
dogmatism without knowledge, whelp-blind
in the frenzy for grace. Listen! The buzz
and thrum of bees probing sepals, spreading
seed. They sting out of necessity or
fear. In the hive, a task and place for all,
no mutiny in nature's harmony.
Out of the hexagon, sweet honey flows.

A welter
    of sarabites
to the hive
    a task of thrum of power
do they sting god
    In the frenzy for grace

Listen

The buzz and thrum of power

A welter of sarabites
    for the purpose of power
  Babel tranced by priestcraft

    whelp-blind
  in their bidding
  in the frenzy of buzz and thrum
bees probing
    begets pistis

dogmatism without
    nature's harmony
  seed sting
    spreading

  Out of bees probing
god devised by trance
    entranced by
  sting
by
stone
  by tranced
    stone

Out of the hexagon, sweet honey flows.
Out of elementary triangles all life forms,
atoms of tetrahedrons, edge upon
edge, clustered into perfect proportion.
Fundamental as air is to nostril,
music to ear, touch to hand.
Cool, smooth topography of marble
breasts or striated ripple of muscle
ripped by knife blades chiselled from harsher rock,
licked by fire's sharp edge, furcal curvatures.
All this will never be written in stone.
Where is truth in covert transformations?
Vessel into chalice, wine into blood,
inflaming persuasion, numbing reason.

Cool
     smooth
music
  to
       nostril

all life chiselled from harsher rock

    licked by knife forms
  atoms of elementary triangles

licked by knife
    all life
    forms
      atoms of
    marble breasts or

ripple of the
    hexagon   numbing
      persuasion
numbing passion
     numbing perfect proportions

    Vessel into chalice wine into chalice
      wine into
        persuasion, numbing
    perfect proportions

into persuasion, sweet
    honey flows

Out

Inflaming persuasion, numbing reason,
behind every portal whisperers lurk.
Let me lead you into the open air
palm branch in outstretched palm, there
we can discuss the dust of the cosmos,
this numinous quintessence unfolding
stars and planets, orbits intersecting
in squares and trines. Gentle Synesius,
Temperance will cradle you in her arms.
My fate churns in thought's vast receptacle,
the soul's spheres and domes, Earth's harmonic mix
of strange with familiar, sempiternal.
Wonder will cradle me until the end,
illume my path to the unbounded edge.

Discuss the soul's sphere
      we can
   discuss the cosmos
this numinous intersecting
   of planet   orbits
     quintessence until
              the end

illume my path to the open
      air

Illume my
  path
     to the dust of soul's
       spheres and planets
     orbit in her arms

    My fate
churns into the soul's
   sphere
       we can discuss the soul's sphere
       we can discuss the open air
palm branch in
 outstretched
   palm

Wonder   will cradle me

      we can discuss
the
   end
     in the open
air

Illume my path to the unbounded edge
where the mesh of being disbands back
to air and ash. Lunes of my flesh rendered
to elements, bit by bit the body
carved away—one, two, three, five—exponents
excruciating—eight, thirteen. Listen—
is that my screech or theirs? Twenty-one crows
in a tree. Caw, caw, claw. Thirty-four—
no more, no more! Detune me no more!
Such silence in this soaring, this sudden
shift in energy a soft buzzing hum.
Nitrians, I forgive your hard, curled claws
of ambition. Pray for *theourgia*,
divinity revealed in abstraction.

     Pray forgive
your hard, curled energy a
   soft buzzing hum

Listen
     is that my
   screech or
  body
carved
 away   one, two, three, five
exponents
        bit by bit
    by
  bit

Pray forgive your hard curled claw

Listen
     is that   my

excruciating   this
     soaring
bit by bit
     by bit by bit by bit by bit by bit by
 bit

the unbounded edge
   where divinity
claws

     Listen
is that
my flesh of being

humming

Unfurling a holy chorus of rage
in immaculate knots, bone spurs of thought
vital as fire is to the body's blood,
wisdom's weapons become fire's desire.
Three gods in one equilateral trick
as hypocrite sun glints off chalices
and gifts of reflection render beauty.
Integers tantalize like wine, like tongues
while I hold your head in my lap and sing.
Entranced by transcendence is how they know
out of the hexagon honey flows
inflaming persuasion, numbing reason.
Illume my path to the unbounded edge
where life emerges and the mind opens.

NOTES ON THE TEXT

I began working on this manuscript in 2010 during a month-long residency at The Wallace Stegner House. It started as a book of poetry based on the work and lives of famous mathematicians and slowly mutated to include other areas of interest—philosophy, surrealism, ecology, politics. The book and section title *Catastrophe Theories* is taken from French mathematician René Thom's study of abrupt transitions or changes in dynamic or gradually evolving systems—ecological systems, for example. His quote at the beginning of this book is from *Topoi, the Categorical Analysis of Logic* (2013) R. Goldblatt.

"Duloxetine Dreams" — The phrase "Wits but a wool gathering" is from Robert Burton's *The Anatomy of Melancholy*, Misery of Scholars Mem. 3. Subs. 15, line 26. Imagery for the poem, aside from dreams, comes from the recent excavation of a fast-food eatery at Pompeii.

"Ode to Alan Turing" — The text in quotations and italicized font are from Turing's *On Computable Numbers, with an Application to the Entscheidungsproblem*.

"Hypatia's Lament" — Hypatia was a revered mathematician, astronomer, philosopher, and teacher, who lived in the turbulent 5th century CE when Christianity was rearing its intolerant head. According to legend and historical sources, she was dragged from her chariot and ripped to pieces (with either oyster shells or roof tiles) by a mob of fanatical Nitrian monks (Deakin 2007). Her death was around the time the great library of Alexandria was burned, destroying centuries of ancient knowledge and leading to the Dark Ages. The phrase "wet nurse of becoming" is from Plato's *Timeaus* (42d, 7). Hypatia was a Neo-Platonist and would have quoted freely from his work. When reading Stephen Hawking's *God Created the Integers* to research some of these poems, I noted that Hypatia was only mentioned in a footnote. I chose an heroic crown of sonnets for its circular, iterative complexity to pay homage to her life, work, and death.

"Markov Echologues" — I wanted a contemporary echo to the formalist poems and ran each sonnet through a Markov Chaining algorithm (often multiple times) from the website Language is a Virus. I edited the poems slightly for length and repetition but kept word choice and format as much as possible. I was astonished by the algorithm's uncanny echo.

The poems subtitled "Dream Phrases" were written after waking up with that phrase in my mind. Often, these phrases were independent of dream imagery, although some is evident in many of the poems in the "Precognitions."

ACKNOWLEDGEMENTS

Some of these poems have been published in the *Aesthetica Creative Writing Annual Magazine, Fractured Ecologies, Golden Handcuffs Review, The Journal of Humanistic Mathematics, Rampike,* and *Release any Words Stuck Inside of You III*. My sincere thanks to the editors.

I am extremely grateful to the Saskatchewan Arts Board for supporting this work. I would like to thank the board of directors of the Wallace Stegner House for a very productive residency. Thank you to the Banff International Research Station for Mathematical Innovation and Discovery and fellow participants in the Creative Writing and Mathematics Workshop for helping me hone many of these poems. Ongoing thanks to St. Peter's Abbey, the Saskatchewan Writers Guild SK Writers/Artist retreats, and the solace and inspiring camaraderie they have provided over the years.

My deep gratitude to Sylvia Legris, Stephanie Strickland, and Phil Hall for their astute editorial comments. Love and thanks to Robert McNealy and Paul Dutton for sharing this journey. Many thanks to Jeanette Lynes, Sheri Benning, Beatriz Hausner, Betsy Rosenwald, Kathleen Whelan, Lisa Pasold, Jennifer K. Dyck, David Lee, Joanne Lyons, Rhona McAdam, Dawna Rose, Terry Billings, Joanne Rochester, Larry Gasper, Hilary Clark, and Steven Ross Smith for advice, support, and intellectual/creative sustenance. Thanks to Maureen Sulyk for ongoing friendship. And thanks to Nancy and Esther for helping me keep body and soul together, or at least within relative proximity.

And, of course, my thanks to Brian and the Anvil Team for their continued support of my work.

REFERENCES

Burton, Robert. *Anatomy of Melancholy* (1621). Eds, Thomas C. Faulkner, Nicolas K. Kiessling, and Rhonda L. Blair, Oxford University Press, 1989.

Deakin, Michael A.B. *Hypatia of Alexandria*. New York: Prometheus Books, 2007.

Goldblatt, Robert. *Topoi, the Categorical Analysis of Logic*. Dover Books on Mathematics, 2013.

Hawking, Stephen. *God Created the Integers*. London, Philadelphia: Running Press, 2005.

Plato. *Timeaus*. Trans. Donald J. Zeyl, Cambridge: Hackett Publishing Company, 2000.

ABOUT THE AUTHOR

Eco-science poet, essayist, and interdisciplinary scholar, Mari-Lou Rowley has published nine collections of poetry, most recently *Unus Mundus* (Anvil Press), which was nominated for three Saskatchewan Book Awards. Rowley's poetry, essays and book chapters have appeared internationally in literary, arts and science-related books and journals, including *Fractured Ecologies* (Denmark), the *Journal of Humanistic Mathematics* (US), and *Aesthetica Magazine*'s (UK) Creative Works Competition. Her multimedia work includes the video-poem *Prairie Surreal* (The Goose). Rowley is currently the Editor of *Grain* magazine and is working on a novel and poetic memoir.